Visiting the Past

Mission San Juan Capistrano

Tristan Boyer Binns

Heinemann Library
Chicago, Illinois

Designed by Wilkinson Design
Photographs by Tristan Boyer Binns
Illustrations by Monique Rea
Printed and bound by Lake Book, Chicago, Illinois, U.S.A.

06 05 43 03 02
10 9 8 7 6 5 4 3 2 1

Library of Congress Cataloging-In-Publication Data
Binns, Tristan Boyer, 1968-
  San Juan Capistrano / Tristan Boyer Binns.
    p. cm. -- (Visiting the past)
Includes bibliographical references and index.
  ISBN 1-58810-272-6 (lib. bdg.)   1-58810-410-9 (pbk. bdg.)
  1. Mission San Juan Capistrano--History--Juvenile literature. 2. San
Juan Capistrano (Calif.)--Social life and customs--Juvenile literature.
3. Juaneño Indians--Missions--California--San Juan
Capistrano--History--Juvenile literature. 4. Spaniards--California--San
Juan Capistrano--History--Juvenile literature. 5.
Franciscans--California--San Juan Capistrano--History--Juvenile
literature. 6. California--History--To 1846--Juvenile literature. [1.
Mission San Juan Capistrano--History. 2. Missions--California. 3.
Juaneño Indians--Missions--California. 4. Indians of North
America--Missions--California. 5. Spaniards--California--History. 6.
California--History--To 1846.] I. Title. II. Series.
  F869.S395 B56 2001
  979.4'96--dc21
                                        2001000842

Acknowledgments
The author and publisher would like to thank Gordon McDonald and Tammye Dunne at Mission San
Juan Capistrano. Special thanks to Father Bill Krekelberg at the Catholic Parish of the Mission Basilica
San Juan Capistrano for his help in the preparation of this book.

Some words in the book appear in bold, **like this.**
You can find out what they mean by looking in the glossary.

Contents

The Spanish Missions 4

The Beginnings of Mission San Juan

　Capistrano 6

Mission San Juan Capistrano 8

From Native American to Neophyte. . . . 10

Religion Every Day 12

Daily Life 14

Growing Food. 16

Cooking and Eating. 18

Working and Making Things 20

Made from Cattle and Sheep 22

Free Time and Celebrations. 24

The End of the Era 26

Time Line. 28

Site Map. 29

Glossary 30

More Books to Read 31

Index 32

The Spanish Missions

After Christopher Columbus began exploring the "New World" in 1492, other European countries rushed to claim land. Leaders of these countries thought they could use the **natural resources** in the New World to make themselves richer. They could trade their goods with the local people and build forts and trading posts for their ships. But people already lived on this land. Groups of Native Americans had lived in North America for thousands of years. They didn't believe in owning land and were confused by the Europeans' claims of ownership. When the Europeans arrived and claimed land on which Native Americans lived, they usually did so without a fight.

Spanish explorers sailed along much of the east and west coasts of North America in the 1500s. They settled present-day Mexico and Florida. In 1542, Juan Rodríguez Cabrillo led the first Spanish expedition to California. He claimed the land for Spain but left immediately. The English explorer Sir Francis Drake explored the California coast in 1579 and claimed the land for Britain, but the British never settled there. Russians started settling the coast of Alaska in the 1700s, and sent explorers as far south as present-day San Francisco. This angered the Spanish, who then began to build their communities in 1769.

The Spanish had a plan to turn Native Americans into Spanish citizens, which would help them protect their claims. Spanish settlers and religious leaders, called **padres,** built missions. Missions were small cities led by padres, with their own industries and farms. Soldiers and a source of supplies supported a mission. The local Native Americans were invited to join the mission, which offered a steady supply of food and safety from attacks from other Indian tribes.

▼ The Spanish would have arrived at a coastline similar to this.

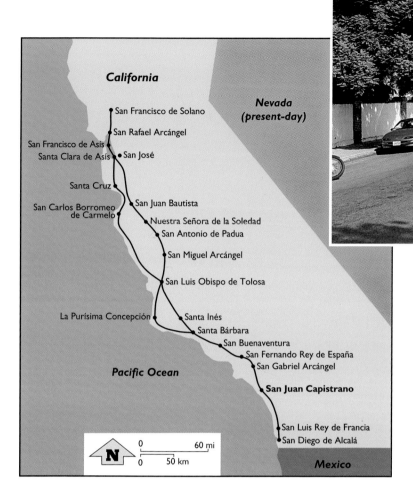

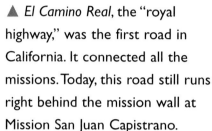

▲ *El Camino Real*, the "royal highway," was the first road in California. It connected all the missions. Today, this road still runs right behind the mission wall at Mission San Juan Capistrano.

In order to join the mission, the Native Americans needed to become **Catholics**. As time went on, those who joined the mission learned the Spanish ways of life. They blended these with their own knowledge and customs. The Spanish plan was to hand the mission over to the new Spanish citizens—the local Native Americans—after ten years. The Spanish settlers would then move to other areas to set up new missions. At its best, this was a good system for several reasons. The Spanish needed only a few people to settle large areas, the Native American people learned a way of life that gave them reliable food, shelter, and income, and there wasn't much warfare. However, this system did destroy the traditional Native American way of life.

A small group of people traveled north from Spanish-owned Mexico to found the missions. The leader of the missions in California was Padre Junípero Serra. He went with Don Gaspar de Portolá, who was the governor of Baja California. In 1769, they founded the mission at San Diego. A year later and 650 miles (1,046 kilometers) north, the next mission was founded at Monterey Bay. Over the years, 21 missions were founded from San Diego in the south to just north of San Francisco, each about a day's journey apart. Many of California's present-day cities have grown around the original missions.

The Beginnings of Mission San Juan Capistrano

The seventh mission to be founded in California was Mission San Juan Capistrano. It was founded in October 1775, but abandoned after a few days when the mission at San Diego was attacked by Native Americans and people became scared. A year later, on November 1, 1776, **Padre** Junípero Serra came back. The mission was moved two years later, when they realized there wasn't enough water in its first location. The new location had flat land for farming and was surrounded by grassy hills for grazing livestock. It was also near the sea, which allowed for fishing and made it easy to reach trading ships. Most importantly, there was fresh water at the site.

Pacific Ocean   mission

▲ The mission at San Juan Capistrano was set back from the sea, on a flat piece of land between the hills.

When the mission was founded, a document was written that listed all of the people and supplies at San Juan Capistrano. There were seventeen people: two padres, six soldiers, a person to look after the mules, two pairs of husbands and wives, and four Native American boys. There was little food and only a few tools to help build the new mission and to farm the land. The people had a fairly large number of animals to raise for food.

The **missionaries** were very religious, and they brought many supplies with which to set up a church. Paintings of religious scenes helped to teach the Native Americans important Bible stories. Fabric for the **altar**, special clothing for the padres, and beautiful ornaments used during mass impressed the Native Americans. A bell was used to call people to worship and work. A special shell was used to **baptize** the new **Catholics**.

Several leather-bound books were used to record the activities of the mission. These records told how many Native Americans were baptized, how many people died, how many marriages were performed, how much food was produced, and how many animals were kept. By 1847, more than 4,500 people had been baptized at the mission. The number of cattle grew from the original 12 to nearly 14,000 by 1820. Between

1797 and 1826, more than 1,000 Native American Catholics lived at Mission San Juan Capistrano, while only six soldiers and two padres lived there. One padre was in charge of religious matters and the other of everyday things. Over time, Native Americans helped with the everyday running of the mission.

▲ On a typical day, the courtyard was bustling with activity. Women and men wove and spun wool and tended to animals, children played, padres taught, and soldiers worked.

Mission San Juan Capistrano

The mission was built like all missions, in Spanish style. It was a small, walled city. At first, the settlers built only a church and living quarters. But over the years, more buildings were added. Soon more living quarters, workshops, kitchens, and storerooms were built on all four sides of the courtyard. These buildings were made from **adobe** bricks. When windows were added, iron bars covered them for safety.

On the buildings facing the courtyard were open-roofed **arcades.** The buildings had no inside hallways, so people walked between them through these arcades. In bad weather or bright sun, people also worked under the protection of the arcade roofs. Two gates allowed entry into the courtyard.

▶ At first, the mission roofs were thatched, or made of dried grasses. When Native Americans burned the roofs at the mission in Santa Barbara with flaming arrows, the Spanish replaced the thatch with clay tiles. The tiles in this photo are rounded because they were shaped over a person's thigh.

The mission was like a farmhouse on a very big farm. Around it were farmlands and **vineyards.** Cattle grazed as far north as present-day Los Angeles. Livestock also lived nearby the mission for everyday needs. Orchards grew near the mission kitchen. By the early 1800s, the mission traded with ships that sailed along the coast. Cow hides and food were traded for iron, cloth, bronze, and copper.

The settlers dug a large pool to hold water just north of the mission. Channels called *zanjas* directed water from the creeks to the mission. All this water was used for cooking, cleaning, watering crops, and drinking.

courtyard   mission buildings

◀ The courtyard had no plants in it; instead, it was hard-packed dirt.

There were soon too many people to all live within the buildings in the mission, so a small village of about 50 adobe huts was built nearby. Native Americans also lived in villages a little farther away.

▲ The arcades led from the buildings to the courtyard.

The mission residents soon learned about earthquakes. A huge stone church was built between 1796 and 1806. But in 1812, an earthquake struck during mass. Forty **neophytes,** or **baptized** Native Americans, couldn't get out before the walls fell and the roof collapsed. To help avoid these kinds of disasters and keep other buildings from collapsing, two **lintels** were used above doors and windows. Walls were built very thickly. **Buttresses** helped hold up the walls. **Foundations** were made from loose stone packed into trenches under the walls. The stone moved with the ground during an earthquake, so the buildings moved too and stayed standing.

▲ This main gate was closed at night with all the others.

◀ Horse manure was mixed with mud and straw to make adobe bricks. Flecks of straw show where the plaster has come off. If water is spilled on the adobe floors, you can still smell the horse manure!

▲ This *zanja* in the courtyard once channeled water to the mission.

9

From Native American to Neophyte

About 15 percent of the Native Americans in California joined a mission and became **Catholic**. This is amazing because at first the Spanish and the Native Americans did not speak the same language. They had to communicate using hand signals. There were many different tribes in California whose members spoke more than 135 languages and followed different customs and traditions. The Native Americans had already established trade routes. None of the tribes farmed much. They didn't need to. They could hunt, fish, and gather plants and seeds for food.

At San Juan Capistrano, the Spanish offered a way of life that appealed to some Native Americans. The Native Americans near San Juan Capistrano were called the Acjachemem. The Spanish called them Juaneños. Although the work in the mission was difficult, it was an easier life for some Acjachemem. Because the residents of the mission farmed crops and raised livestock, there was always food. People didn't have to fear going hungry.

The Acjachemem were interested in the new rituals and processions of the Spanish Catholics, with their fine fabrics and

▲ The Acjachemem lived in small round huts made from reeds.

▼ A main food of the Acjachemem was acorns, which had to be gathered and prepared. They were ground on stones like this one, where women would grind and talk together.

beautiful pictures. So over a short time, many Acjachemem decided to join the mission. It took between six and twelve months to become a Catholic. First the Acjachemem had to learn the basic beliefs of Christianity. When they had accepted these beliefs as their own, they were **baptized**. After that they were called **neophytes**.

Some Acjachemem at the mission chose not to become Catholics, but they were welcome at the mission anyway because other family members were Christian. It is part of the teachings of the Catholic church that a person can't be forced into becoming a Catholic. But once Native Americans joined the religion and the mission, they would be brought back if they ran away. The **padres** thought it was good for the neophytes to keep learning about Christianity, and they had to be in the mission to keep learning. The Spanish were also afraid that a neophyte who ran away might tell an enemy about the mission's defenses. This seldom happened at San Juan Capistrano. Problems were created at other missions, however, when neophytes wished to leave. Usually this happened when there was a poor harvest and there was a shortage of food.

▲ This is a statue of Padre Serra and a Native American boy. Padre Serra was known for being kind to the Native Americans and supporting them.

◀ The Acjachemem made baskets, like these. The baskets were used for many things, such as cooking and storage. They were sometimes even used as hats.

◀ This is the stone font, or basin, used for baptisms.

11

Every day, church bells rang so that people would know when to eat, pray, and work. Each day began with prayer and mass for the **padres** and the **neophytes**. The padres spent much of their time on religious matters and saying private prayers. The padres also spent time teaching the Native Americans about Christianity. A group would gather around a padre in the courtyard or in the church. When in the church, the padre could use the paintings to help explain Bible stories. On special days they said prayers and sang songs. On Sundays, everyone spent more time in church.

During most of the mission's life, most worshipping was done in the **adobe** church, which was completed in 1782.

▲ The gilded, or gold, altarpiece in the Serra Chapel was added in the 1900s. At first, there were just spaces in the wall filled with silver candlesticks and statues. The wall paintings are accurate copies of the originals.

Because Padre Serra said mass there when he visited in 1783, it is now known as the Serra Chapel. It is the oldest building still standing in California. The floor was dirt, and there were no pews, or benches, on which to sit. Women brought cushions to sit on. The walls inside were painted with bright, complicated designs. Even the ceiling was decorated. The style of the paintings grew from a mix of Spanish and Native American cultures. The building was narrow because the ceiling had to be supported by solid wood beams. Very long wood beams

◀ The stone church was very big. Its walls stood where there is only rubble today.

◀ Today, work is being done to **stabilize** the church remains. The column on the right is modern, made to replace one about to fall down. Workers are using steel rods to tie the stones together in the dome.

▲ The **replica** of the stone church shows what it would have looked like before it fell. The bells hung in the bell tower, the tallest part of the building.

▲ The interior of the replica stone church shows what the original painted walls would have looked like. Light fills this open area.

were not available. The church is long because by 1790, more than 700 people needed to worship in it. It couldn't be made wider so more was added at the north end. Behind the chapel lies the cemetery. More than 3,000 people are buried there, mostly Native Americans.

The stone church was a beautiful building with seven domes on top. It was very big, built to serve the ever-growing mission. It had a vaulted, or arched, stone roof and a tall bell tower. The walls were decorated with beautiful painted designs. Mission San Juan Capistrano was called the "jewel of the missions" because sunlight reflected off the stone church and it shone like a jewel to sailors on the Pacific Ocean. The people of the mission were very proud of the church. But the earthquake in 1812 destroyed it and killed 40 worshippers inside.

Today, there is a copy of the stone church at the the mission. It is bigger than the original, but otherwise the same. It gives people an idea of how it must have felt to be inside the original church.

► This wall painting high on the dome of the stone church is original.

◄ Goods were shipped to the mission in crates. This booth in the church was made from one of those crates.

Daily Life

The residents at the mission had a daily **routine.** The **neophytes** lived away from the **padres** and the soldiers. They even had different kitchens. Most neophytes lived in villages outside the mission walls, some far away at the *ranchos* where they looked after the farms. Some lived inside the mission, like young unmarried women. Children were considered to be adults at age ten, but some children were married when they were younger. Most of the Acjachemem went to visit their home villages regularly, especially during busy times like the acorn harvest.

Spanish soldiers lived in a building called a barracks. Usually six to twelve men lived and ate there. They kept their weapons, ammunition, and explosives in a special place called a magazine, which was attached to the same building.

At sunrise, the padres rang the bells. People made and ate breakfast and then worked until noon. Adults built buildings, made crafts, and farmed the fields. Children went to school in the morning. After lunch at noon, people had a rest, or *siesta*. Then they worked more. Children helped with the crafts, tended animals, and helped grow and cook food. The evenings were free for playing and talking. Some days there were religious services or festivals and plays.

◀ The soldiers' barracks shows how the soldiers slept and ate. Their beds were made of strips of hides or ropes tightened on a wood frame. They slept on furs.

brazier

▶ The fireplace in the padres' quarters was added much later. The padres used **braziers** that held charcoal to heat their rooms.

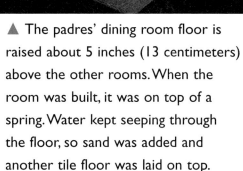

▼ These guest rooms were next to the padres' rooms. Some guests stayed in the soldiers' barracks.

▲ The padres' dining room floor is raised about 5 inches (13 centimeters) above the other rooms. When the room was built, it was on top of a spring. Water kept seeping through the floor, so sand was added and another tile floor was laid on top.

Padres were supposed to live "in community," which means they should live in a group. Missions always had two padres so they could live in a small community. This gave them another Spanish leader to talk to and make plans with. The padres had a room to live and sleep in and a separate dining room. Even so, some padres found life too hard in the missions and went back to Mexico or Spain.

Many guests visited the missions as they traveled through California. They were always offered food and a bed to sleep in. Padres welcomed visitors, who often brought news from the outside world.

▶ The courtyard, which was originally dirt, was busy as people spun wool, wove baskets, and learned Spanish. Padres taught religious classes here as well.

One of the important daily jobs of the **neophytes** was to grow food to feed all the mission people. Crops were also traded for goods they needed. The livestock produced much of the mission's trade goods, including hides and **tallow** for candles and soap.

The mission buildings were at the center of a large farm. Some gardens and orchards were next to the kitchens or just outside the walls. The big fields were farther away. Some animals, such as chickens and doves, were kept at the mission. Herds of large animals grazed in pastures around the mission. Some cattle grazed as far as Costa Mesa, which is 22 miles (35 kilometers) away. It was a very long walk or ride in mission times.

People who tended the animals and fields close to the mission lived in the villages nearby. Those who looked after the distant fields and herds lived in **ranchos.** Even children helped to produce food.

▲ Olive trees like these gave the mission olives and olive oil.

▲ There was a pool near here just behind the mission, which gave water for **irrigation** to the fields by the mission. Animals were also kept penned near here.

◀ Cattle were branded with the mission's branding iron.

In the orchard, there was a watchtower made of tall poles. A Native American boy would perch in the tower and make noises to scare off the birds trying to eat the fruit.

People grew fruit in the orchards and vineyards. They ate a variety of fruits, including dates, olives, grapes, peaches, pears, and figs. Tall walls kept neighboring Native Americans from picking the mission fruit. Toilets were located in the orchards. Waste ran down from there into the river.

Food was stored in a pantry. Supplies were placed in baskets and jars for storage. The pantry was not a big room because not much storage space was needed. Fresh food was available most of the year because the climate was so good.

Usually, the harvests were large and the herds of animals grew quickly. But after the earthquake in 1812, this changed. Weeds, diseases, floods, and drought made it harder to keep feeding all the people. Fewer neophytes joined each year, and the total number of neophytes began to drop.

▲ The woodwork in this pantry is original. The balcony above the room is a good storage place for jars.

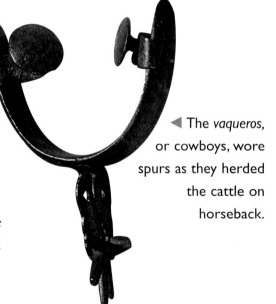

◀ The *vaqueros,* or cowboys, wore spurs as they herded the cattle on horseback.

FOOD HARVESTED, SHOWN IN FANEGAS — I FANEGA=100 LBS. (45 KG)				
Year	Wheat	Barley	Corn	Beans	Garbanzo beans
1792	2,835	60	2,000	50	0
1811	5,000	1,900	2,020	206	9.5

LIVESTOCK BY HEAD					
Year	Cattle	Sheep	Goats	Pigs	Horses	Mules
1783	430	305	830	40	32	11
1810	14,000	16,000	215	182	740	126

Cooking and Eating

Every morning, women lit fires in the kitchen and began to make breakfast for up to 1,000 **neophytes**. The kitchen was outdoors, but covered by a tile roof called an *enramada*. It wasn't very large. In fact, it was called the "little kitchen." Cookstoves had flat tops on which to cook. Ovens were shaped like beehives. Fires were built inside to heat the cooking space, then swept out when the space was hot. Bread was then placed and baked in the empty space. Food was cooked in pottery jars and stored in pottery or baskets. Because the mission had furnaces to work metal, metal pots and hot plates were used for cooking as well.

In the morning and evening, people ate *atole*. This is a thin soup made from ground corn. At lunch, people ate *pozole,* which is atole with meat and vegetables added. Most of the year, there was also fresh or dried fruit and bread. Neophytes also had snacks between meals, like fruit, nuts, and seeds. Eating three meals a day year-round was a big deal at the time, especially three nutritious and tasty meals.

▲ Soot marks from the beehive-shaped oven run up the wall in the padres' kitchen.

▲ This cookstove in the padres' kitchen has a metal hot plate on top. Pots were heated on top of the hot plate.

◄ The padres' indoor kitchen was almost as big as the little kitchen outdoors, but fed many fewer people each day. Food stored in dishes and jars was placed on the shelves and benches along the wall.

▲ The women in the little kitchen cooked up to 3,000 meals each day.

▲ These millstones ground corn and pressed olives.

Grinding corn was an important job, since most of what people ate was based on corn. There was a **gristmill** near the little kitchen. Olives were also milled, pressed for their oil.

The **padres** ate the same food and on the same schedule as the neophytes. But only men could cook for the padres. The cooks were usually young men who wanted to become leaders themselves. They learned much by spending time working for and watching the padres. The padres had a kitchen of their own near their quarters. It was in a room in one of the **arcades**. The room had two ovens and two stoves, but only one chimney in the middle of the ceiling.

▼ The cookstoves in the little kitchen are the same size as those in the padres' kitchen.

▲ This brick drain was uncovered in 1934. The rest of the little kitchen was found afterwards.

19

Working and Making Things

Mission leaders were also interested in teaching **neophytes** special skills and crafts. Spanish craftsmen traveled to all the missions for three to five years, teaching their crafts. A craftsman stayed at each mission long enough to teach some of the neophytes his skills. Then he moved on to the next mission. Spanish craftspeople taught people at Mission San Juan Capistrano how to work iron and tin, make wheels, build with wood, weave and dye cloth, work leather, and make pottery. Workshops were set up around the mission grounds for crafts that needed large equipment.

The metalworking furnace at the mission is the oldest in California. Workers used it to make iron, copper, and brass. A blacksmith helped shape the iron into useful tools and horseshoes. Liquid iron could also be poured into molds to make other objects.

Carpenters and masons, people who build with brick and stone, helped to keep the mission growing. These men were always building. They also fixed the older buildings at the mission.

▶ The furnace is right next to the dyeing vats. There were three chimneys for the fires that kept the metal hot.

▶ The workshop area is behind the west wing of the mission. Each work activity took place near the others.

dyeing vats   leather stretching circle   tanning vats

furnace

tallow area

▶ The blacksmith's area is next to the furnace. Men were usually blacksmiths.

By 1787, mission workers had built a kiln—an oven used to fire clay and make pottery—just north of the mission. When clay gets very hot, it turns into a kind of stone. Fired clay bricks don't melt like **adobe** when they get wet. Fired clay tiles make good waterproof roofs. Fired clay pots are also useful in cooking and holding water and other liquids. The Native Americans in this area did not know how to make pottery before the Spanish arrived. They learned very quickly when the tools were given to them. Today, a street called *Horno,* or oven, Street runs where the kiln once was.

▼ This crucible, or container, was used to melt metal in the furnace. A blacksmith made the iron candlestick next to it.

Metal crucible used in metal furnaces at ...sh missions.

Near the workshops, archaeologists have found what they believe is the infirmary, or hospital. People with **contagious diseases** came here to be treated and to stop them from passing their illness on to others. Most of the diseases were introduced by accident by the Spanish when they settled the area. The local people had no **resistance** to European diseases.

◀ Archaeologists think this is the site of the infirmary. The big wooden tables have screens in them. They are used to sift the dirt dug out of the ground so small artifacts can be saved.

▶ Archaeologists carefully plot the areas in which they are digging. String grids help them do this.

Made from Cattle and Sheep

The large numbers of sheep and cattle at the mission meant there was always plenty of wool, meat, **tallow,** and hides. Many of the mission workshops were built to make these things. Tallow was made by boiling the fat from sheep and cattle in big vats, or tubs. Tallow was made into candles, soap, grease, and ointments. It was also traded for supplies the mission needed.

Candles were made by dipping wicks made of cotton string into melted tallow many times. Soap was more difficult to make. First ashes from fires were soaked in water. This made lye, a harsh chemical. When the lye and the tallow were carefully cooked together, they formed a soft, mushy soap. It didn't smell good, but it cleaned people and clothes and anything else that needed to be washed.

▲ The barrel on the left was used to soak ashes to make lye for soap. The big cauldrons, or pots, were used to boil fat into tallow, and then to heat the tallow to make into soap and candles.

▲ The tallow workshop is at the end of the **arcade,** on the courtyard.

◀ These two huge vats were used to tan hides into leather.

Tanning hides to make leather was another important craft. Cattle hides were soaked in a deep vat filled with water and salt or lime. This cleaned the hides. Then the hides went into the next vat to be tanned. Ground bark from oak trees or acorns made the tannic acid that was mixed with water to tan the hides. The tanned hides were then stretched in a brick circle and rubbed with grease and tallow to make them smooth and soft. When they dried they were done.

Sheep's wool was washed and spun into yarn. Simple spindles were made from potatoes or other vegetables with small sticks stuck into them. Other spindles were made with longer sticks. The spindles were spun on the floor or the spinner's thigh to help draw the bunched wool out into a long yarn. Much later on, people used spinning wheels to make the process easier and quicker.

▶ The spindle on the left uses a potato to help spin wool. The one on the right is a long, heavy stick.

Wool yarn was woven into cloth on simple looms. Looms were made by stretching lengths of wool between the floor and ceiling, or between two pieces of wood. Yarn was woven under and over the wool lengths to make a strong cloth. Finer yarn was made into clothes, and thicker yarn into rugs and blankets. Workers wove and spun in many places— in the courtyard, under the arcades, or in their homes. Before they had wool cloth, the Acjachemem made clothes from fibers found in plants. Wool was stronger, softer, and easier to work with. Vats near the tallow working area were probably used to dye the wool different colors. Workers made their own dyes from plants and animal parts. Both men and women spun, wove, and dyed wool.

▼ A drain ran from this circular area, used to stretch hides, past the tanning vats.

▶ These vats were probably used to dye wool. The vats run like steps down to the leather-stretching circle.

Free Time and Celebrations

Mission residents had free time each day. Children loved to play together and with their parents, just like children today. Children used sticks and round stones to play games, and they made rattles from animal horns. Guessing games and catching games were fun. **Neophyte** children and adults learned to sing in Latin, which was the language used for **Catholic** masses and ceremonies, and in Spanish. They also learned to play instruments like the guitar, flute, and violin. Guests wrote about how beautiful the choirs at the missions sounded.

Bullfights were popular with children and adults. These were held in the courtyard. People showed off their skills with the animals and competed against each other. Everyone watching the events sat on the **arcade** roofs to see well and stay out of danger! Sometimes a dance was held in the courtyard.

Religious celebrations were very important at the mission. There were feasts and special services on saints' days. The biggest celebrations were saved for St. Joseph's Day on March 19, Easter, and Christmas. St. Joseph is the patron saint of all missions, so his feast day was special.

▼ People sat on the roofs and watched events in the courtyard below.

Starting at the beginning of the Christmas season, there were special church services with choirs and musicians singing special **chants.** On Christmas Eve, people rang the bells for a long time and fired rockets into the sky. A special mass was said and there was singing and music. A group of people dressed in fine clothes paraded around the mission. Finally there was the *Pastorela,* or Nativity play. Today, Nativity plays tell the Christian Christmas story of the birth of Jesus, and how he was visited by shepherds and other people who brought him gifts. Back then at Mission San Juan Capistrano, the Nativity play told about how the devil tried to stop the shepherds from going to see baby Jesus after he was born.

▲ The Serra Chapel saw many religious celebrations.

◀ The bells rang out on special days, to draw people to the church. The bells were hung in the *campanario* in 1813, after the stone church's bell tower was destroyed. A *campanario* is a bell tower that stands by itself. The small bells are originals, but the big ones are replicas.

25

The End of the Era

In 1821, Mexico won its independence from Spain and took control of California. But Mexico did not rule California very well and often failed to send the supplies it had promised. The missions kept the area going because of their well-organized networks that provided food and work. It was illegal for the missions to trade with merchant ships, but they did so anyway. This trading helped them to get the supplies they needed.

New settlers in California were jealous of the land and riches that the missions had. These people started *ranchos,* or farms. Instead of the church running a large farming operation, one family would own the *rancho* and pay workers to help them grow food and raise animals. Partly because of pressure from these settlers, and partly because the Mexican government thought the **neophytes** should have land of their own, the missions were taken away from the **Catholic** Church in 1833. The Spanish idea of turning local natives into Spanish citizens had worked well in Mexico, so the Mexicans thought it would work in California.

The neophytes were secularized, or removed from religious life. Many protested, and wanted to stay at the missions. Some took the land offered to them and started their own farms.

▲ Inside the stone church, workers are trying to stabilize the walls. The red grid helps them identify where everything is now.

▼ Workers have tried to **stabilize** the remains of the stone church for a long time. About one hundred years ago, the **adobe** bricks on the right were added. More recently, the columns were replaced. The original parts that are left are still strong.

◀ Concrete and steel **buttresses** have been added to stabilize the buildings and walls in case of earthquakes.

▲ Special events on the grounds today draw visitors to the mission and help pay for repairs.

But much of the mission land was not offered to the Native Americans. Instead, it went to the new settlers. Most Native Americans left the area or went to work on the new *ranchos*. The chapel became the new church, and the **padres** were given rooms. All the other buildings were sold. At San Juan Capistrano, some parts of buildings were sold, including roof tiles. This caused many of the buildings to fall down.

After the United States took control of California in 1846, the Catholic Church asked for the mission lands back. A number of missions asked that land be given to the Native Americans. This was a confusing time when many people claimed land rights.

However, few Native Americans received land at San Juan Capistrano. Finally, in 1865, President Abraham Lincoln signed papers returning the mission buildings and 10.5 acres (4.25 hectares) of land to the Catholic Church. The mission buildings needed a lot of work. Starting in 1896, a group called the Landmarks Club helped with repairs. Priests living at the mission, along with other people, have worked to rebuild areas and keep the buildings safe ever since.

27

Time Line

1492	Christopher Columbus sails to the New World
1542	Juan Rodríguez Cabrillo leads expedition and claims California for Spain
1579	Sir Francis Drake claims California for Britain
1602	Spanish expedition led by Sebastián Vizcaíno visits California again
1700s	Russians settle parts of Alaska and later send explorers into California
1769	Padre Junípero Serra and Don Gaspar de Portolá begin founding missions in California
1775	First mission at San Juan Capistrano founded
1776	November 1: permanent mission founded at San Juan Capistrano
1778	location of mission moved closer to water supply
1782	Serra Chapel in use, courtyard in use
1787	Kilns in use for firing clay bricks, roof tiles, and pots
1790	Serra Chapel extended to allow more worshippers
1796	Stone church building begun
1797–1826	More than 1,000 Native American **Catholics** living at mission
1806	Stone church completed
1812	Earthquake ruins stone church, kills 40 worshippers
1813	Church bells hung in the *campanario*
1821	Mexico takes control of California
1833	Secularization of all California missions
1865	Abraham Lincoln signs papers giving the missions back to the Catholic Church
1896	Landmarks Club forms and begins to help repair and **stabilize** San Juan Capistrano

*S*ite *Map*

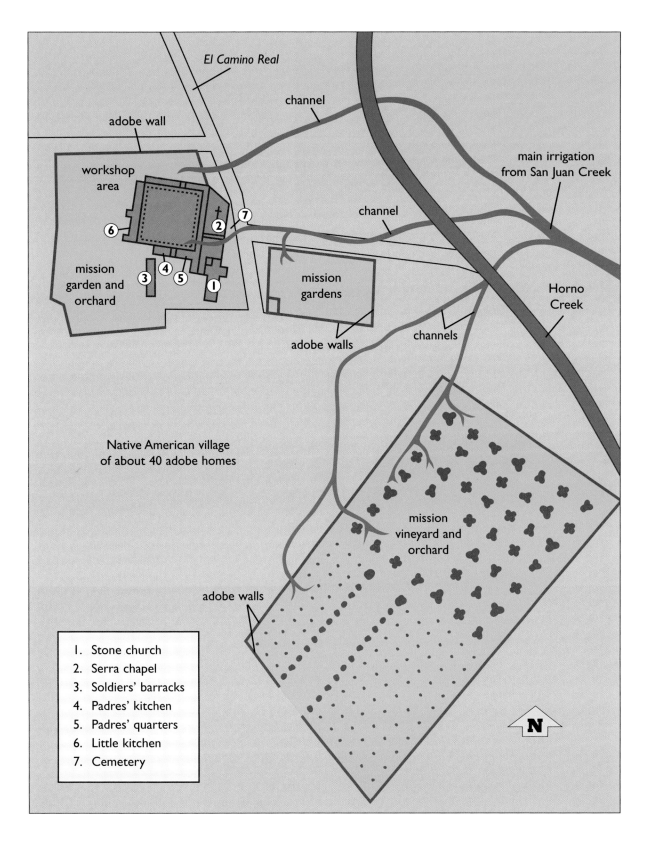

El Camino Real

channel

adobe wall

workshop area

main irrigation from San Juan Creek

channel

⑥

⑦

②

mission garden and orchard

③ ④ ⑤ ①

mission gardens

Horno Creek

adobe walls

channels

Native American village of about 40 adobe homes

mission vineyard and orchard

adobe walls

1. Stone church
2. Serra chapel
3. Soldiers' barracks
4. Padres' kitchen
5. Padres' quarters
6. Little kitchen
7. Cemetery

N

Glossary

adobe mixture of mud, straw, and a binder like horse manure, used to make bricks

altar special area at the front of a church

arcade covered walkway

baptize ceremony in most Christian religions in which new members are welcomed into the church

brazier pan that can be moved around easily and holds hot coals for heat

buttress wings sticking out at right angles from a building, designed to help hold the walls up and make them stronger

Catholic person who believes in the Catholic Christian religion

chant song in which words or syllables are sung in the same tone

contagious disease disease that can be spread by contact between people

foundation base, or part of a building, usually underground, that supports a building above it

gristmill mill for grinding grain

irrigation watering crops by using ditches, pipes, or canals

lintel horizontal part above a window or door that supports the wall above

missionary person who tries to convince others to join their religion

natural resource anything found in nature that can be used by people

neophyte on a mission, Native American baptized into the Catholic Church

padre Catholic priest at a mission

rancho ranch, or farm

replica copy of something, usually very accurate

resistance power to fight something off

routine to always do something the same way

stabilize make sturdy or stop something from falling down

tallow animal fat boiled down and then used to make candles and soap

tanning process of turning raw animal hides into leather

vineyard area where grapevines are planted

More Books to Read

Edgar, Kathleen. *Mission San Juan Capistrano.* New York: Rosen Publishing Group, 2000.

Faber, Gail. *Whispers Along the Mission Trail.* Alamo, Calif.: Magpie Publications, 1986

Faber, Gail. *Whispers from the First Californians: A Story of California's First People.* Alamo, Calif.: Magpie Publications, 1994.

Lemke, Nancy. *Missions of the Southern Coast (California Missions).* Minneapolis, Minn.: Lerner Publications, 1996.

Nelson, Libby, and Kari A. Cornell. *Projects & Layouts: California Missions.* Minneapolis, Minn.: Lerner Publications, 1997.

Van Steenwyk, Elizabeth. *The California Missions.* Danbury, Conn.: Franklin Watts, 1998.

Index

acorns 14, 23
adobe 8, 9, 12, 21, 26
animals 6, 8, 10, 14, 16, 17, 22–23, 24, 26
arcades 8, 9, 19, 22, 24
art 12, 13

barracks 14, 15
bells 6, 12, 14, 25
Britain 4

Cabrillo, Juan Rodríguez 4
Catholic Church (Catholics, Catholicism)
    5, 10, 11, 24, 26, 27
cemetery 13
children 6, 14, 16, 24
churches 9, 12, 13
Columbus, Christopher 4
contagious diseases 21
Costa Mesa 16
courtyard 8, 12, 24
crafts 20

de Portolá, Don Gaspar 5
Drake, Sir Francis 4

earthquakes 9, 13, 17
El Camino Real 5

farming 6, 10, 16
food 6, 8, 11, 15, 16, 17, 18–19, 26

harvest 11, 14, 17
hospital (infirmary) 21

kiln 21

Landmarks Club 27
languages 10, 24
leather tanning 20, 22–23

Lincoln, President Abraham 27
Los Angeles 8

men 6, 19, 20, 23
metalworking 20
Mexico 4, 5, 15, 26
Monterey Bay 5
music 24, 25

Native Americans
    Acjachemem 10, 11, 14
    Juaneño 10
    neophytes 9, 11, 12, 14, 16, 17, 18, 19,
        20, 24, 26

padres 4, 6, 11, 12, 14, 15, 18, 19, 27
play 24
pottery 20, 21

ranchos 14, 16, 26, 27
religion 6, 10, 11, 12–13, 24, 25, 26
Russia 4

San Diego 5, 6
San Francisco 4
Santa Barbara 8
Serra Chapel 12, 13, 25
Serra, Padre Junípero 5, 6, 11, 12
soldiers 4, 6, 7, 14, 15
Spain 4, 15, 26

tallow 20, 22, 23
toilets 17
trade 4, 6, 8, 10, 26

women 6, 12, 14, 18, 19, 23
wool (weaving) 15, 23
workshops 8, 20, 21, 22